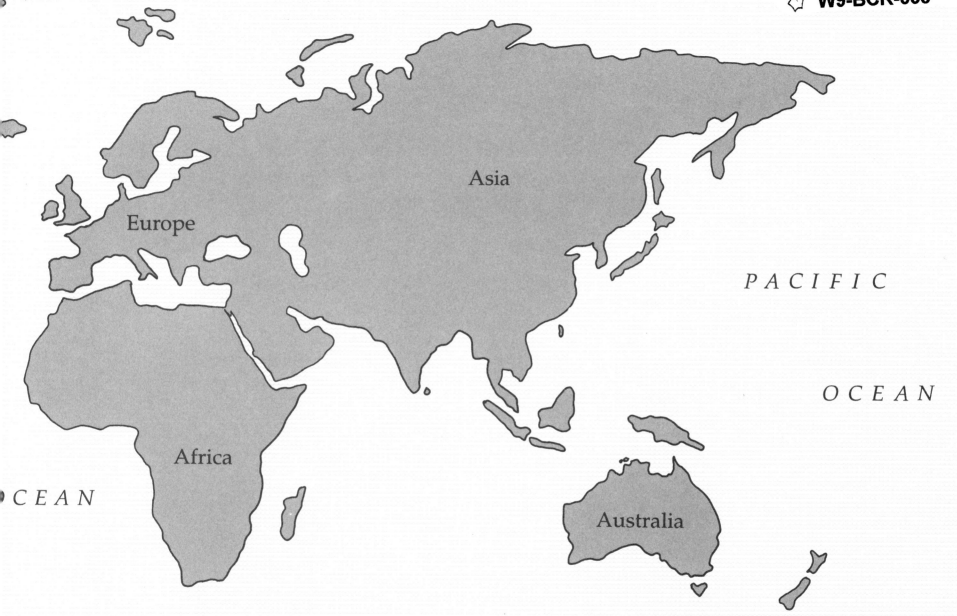

Asia

Europe

PACIFIC

Africa

OCEAN

OCEAN

Australia

AMAZON BASIN
VANISHING CULTURES

Jan Reynolds

Harcourt Brace & Company

San Diego   New York   London

Copyright © 1993 by Jan Reynolds

Library of Congress Cataloging-in-Publication Data
Reynolds, Jan, 1956–
Amazon Basin: vanishing cultures/Jan Reynolds.–1st ed.
p.   cm.–(Vanishing cultures series)
Summary: Describes, in text and photographs, the
vanishing culture of the Yanomama, a primitive group
that lives in the Amazon Territory of Venezuela.
ISBN 0-15-202831-5(hc.) — ISBN 0-15-202832-3(pbk.)
1. Yanomama Indians–Juvenile literature. [I. Yanomama
Indians. 2. Indians of South America. 3. Amazon River
Region–Social life and customs.] I. Title. II. Series.
F2520.I.Y3R45   1993
306'.089'982–dc20   92-21089

First edition
A B C D E   A B C D E (pbk.)

Printed in Singapore

*To my love, Stephen,
and all those in love
around the world
—J. R.*

*To take the photographs in this book, the author used two
35mm cameras with 20mm, 35mm, 105mm, and 180mm lenses.
The display type and text type were set in Palatino by the
Photocomposition Center, Harcourt Brace & Company,
San Diego, California.
Color separations were made by Bright Arts, Ltd., Singapore.
Printed and bound by Tien Wah Press, Singapore
Production supervision by Warren Wallerstein and Ginger Boyer
Designed by Camilla Filancia*

The Yanomama live in the Amazon rain forest, the largest jungle on earth. For half the year little rain falls, but during the other half it rains heavily, day after day. Deep in this rain forest, the Yanomama build large circular huts from grass and wood with roofs that are open in the center. Many extended families live together in one hut. At night they sleep in hammocks around small cooking fires, and during the day they tend gardens, fish in the rivers, and hunt in the jungle.

But their ancient way of life is disappearing. The rain forest is considered valuable by many people who come to mine gold and clear the forest for their own use. Because of this, the Yanomama are leaving their homes and their land.

We are all part of the same human family, and like the Yanomama, we depend on the land and water to live. The Yanomama believe that everything has a spirit and is alive. They care for their land and believe that the spirits of the land will care for them. Perhaps we should take a look at the Yanomama's relationship with the rain forest before the Yanomama vanish forever.

As the moon shines over the Mavaca River in the Amazon Basin, a young Yanomama boy named Tuwenowa sits with his family by the evening fire.

While Tuwenowa's uncle and mother roast plantains, a type of banana, for their evening meal, his grandfather swings in his hammock, telling stories.

"Long ago, when the Yanomama danced, we painted our faces and bodies with the designs and patterns we saw every day in the jungle. We also decorated our hair with the soft, white down feathers we collected from birds. The jungle has always been part of us, and we have always been part of the jungle."

Nose and lip plugs, or sticks, are a form of decoration, too.

"Dancing together, we celebrated life in the heart of the wild jungle. We followed a song leader who would sing *heris,* songs that tell stories about hunting or fishing. Then, all together, we would sing the song leader's words back to him as we danced."

Listening to his grandfather tell stories into the night, Tuwenowa falls asleep, rocking gently in his hammock with his mother.

In the morning, Tuwenowa helps his mother while his father visits relatives at another village down the river. Tuwenowa puts dried plantains in a basket for her to grind and mix with water to make a soft food for his baby sister to eat.

Plantains are a common food for the Yanomama and are part of every meal. This fruit can be prepared in many different ways, but most often it is roasted.

Mother carries baby sister while collecting plantains.

After breakfast, mother says it is time to gather more plantains from their garden in the jungle. To collect the fruit, she pulls on the leaves and branches of the plantain tree, bringing the plantains into reach. Then she uses her large knife, called a machete, to cut them free.

Tuwenowa's older brother, Yamokonawe, also comes to help collect the plantains. He has been at the *kapok* tree and is eating the sweet insides of a seedpod. Tuwenowa loves to eat kapok, too. But he is too young to climb the tree, so his brother gathers the sweet treat for him.

After helping their mother in the garden, Tuwenowa's older brother decides to teach him how to use a bow and arrow. The Yanomama do not raise animals for food. If they want to have meat for dinner, they must hunt the deer, tapir, and other wild animals that live in the jungle.

Yamokonawe makes Tuwenowa his very own arrow to practice with.

Tuwenowa's older brother is able to draw back a strong wooden bow that is taller than he is. He shows Tuwenowa how he lays the arrow's feathers next to his cheek so he can look straight down the shaft to his target. Trying to imitate his brother, Tuwenowa struggles to draw his smaller bow.

Hunting is an important skill, so the boys practice for a long time. When Tuwenowa is able to draw his bow and shoot an arrow straight, they decide to take their bows and arrows to fish in the shallow, muddy waters of a nearby swamp.

With so much sun and so little rain at this time of year, the water is hot. The swamp pond will soon be too dry for good fishing, but right now there are plenty of fish. Even though the pond will dry up, the Yanomama know that when the rainy season comes, the pond will be filled once again with water and fish for them to catch.

Tuwenowa's mother and others are already at the swamp using handwoven baskets to fish with. She will draw her basket across the pond's bottom, then lift it quickly to see if she has caught any fish.

Tuwenowa's mother with a fishing basket

Tuwenowa's older brother shows him how to use a bow and arrow instead of a basket. He sees something moving in the water and shoots, hoping to catch a delicious fish for his family to eat for their dinner.

The next day, Tuwenowa travels with his family down the river in their boat made from a large tree that has been hollowed out. The rain forest is criss-crossed with rivers the Yanomama use for traveling through the dense jungle.

He is going to see his father and the relatives his father has been visiting. As Tuwenowa and his family paddle down the river, they pass the homes, called *shaponos,* of other Yanomama families. Some shaponos are empty because the people are on *wayumi,* looking for food, moving through the jungle, hunting and gathering.

It is not long before Tuwenowa sees some friends playing on the bank of the river in a boat, just like the one his family is in.

The children are happy to see Tuwenowa and his family and will take them to the shapono where Tuwenowa's father is staying.

Tuwenowa's father is a shaman, a man of knowledge and strong spirit, just like his father before him. He has been staying at the village to help the people prepare for a ceremony to honor a relative who has died.

A cord around the climber's feet helps him grip the tree.

The people of the village have been busy gathering food for everyone who will be attending the ceremony.

Some climbed high into the trees to get *rasha,* a deep red peach palm fruit.

While the adults are busy preparing for the ceremony, the children have time to play. One of Tuwenowa's friends has found something good to eat, and she calls to the others to follow her.

The children rush through the thick, green, tangle of the jungle. They come to a tree where a bunch of hard pods hang among long, thin leaves. Using a stick, the children knock the pods down. The sweet liquid inside these pods is a treat shared by everyone.

One of the boys shows his friends his special arrow for hunting birds. It has a tip with many prongs.

In a large garden, just like the one Tuwenowa and his family have, the boy sees a bird on top of an old, dead tree. He tells the others to wait as he quietly sneaks up to shoot. But the bird is too alert and quickly flies away.

In the afternoon the jungle becomes hot, and Tuwenowa and his friends decide to go for a swim. They walk to a stream that comes up out of the ground—it's their favorite swimming spot. Swinging on vines, they fly out over the stream before letting go and dropping into the cool water.

For fun, some of the children paint themselves with the crushed, sticky *onoto* seeds they collected while playing in the jungle.

Later in the afternoon, older family members come down to the stream where the children are swimming. It is time for everyone to decorate themselves for the start of the ceremony.

Black paint is made by mixing onoto seed juice with wood ashes.

Everything they need they find in the jungle: feathers for their hair and liquid from seeds to paint their bodies. Like the Yanomama of long ago, Tuwenowa and his friends decorate themselves with the designs and patterns they see every day.

Soon, young and old gather at the edge of the jungle around the shapono to begin singing their heris and dancing to the songs.

Tuwenowa and his friends whirl and shout behind the song leader, dancing in circles round and round the shapono under the late afternoon sun. For the Yanomama, losing a family member is sad, but life is joyful. As they mourn the passing of their relative, they also celebrate life.

By a fire deep inside the shapono, Tuwenowa's father is also getting ready. As the shaman, he mixes the ashes of the dead relative with fruit and water. In the morning, after the people have danced through the night, the closest family members will drink this mixture. The Yanomama believe that drinking a dead relative's ashes allows the life or spirit to live on with them.

When Tuwenowa gets tired, his father holds him. Together they watch their friends and family perform the dances as the Yanomama have for as long as anyone can remember on the edge of the river, deep in the jungle.

Tuwenowa is proud to be a Yanomama, and he hopes to someday become a shaman like his father and his grandfather before him.

I sat in the copilot's seat, my gear filling the back of the small plane, while Capitano and I flew hour after hour over the dense jungle of the Amazon Territory of Venezuela. The Amazon River Basin is the largest tropical rain forest in the world, about the size of Australia, and I was heading deep into the interior to live with the Yanomama, the largest group of primitive people still remaining on earth.

"Don't panic if you lose your way," Capitano said over the roar of the engine. "The jungle is so thick, you cannot see the sun to give you any direction. Stay near the river—let it be your guide!" After dropping me off in a clearing with all my provisions, including a portable kayak, Capitano zoomed his plane down and buzzed me, furiously waving good-bye. Suddenly, I was alone.

The rain cooled my sweat-streaked skin as I drifted down-river to the confluence of the Orinoco and Mavaca rivers. Although it was early March and still considered the dry season, the rains that normally start in April, dropping one hundred twenty inches annually, had already begun.

When I reached the confluence of the rivers, my first con-tact with the Yanomama led to my meeting two doctors from Spain and Cuba—the Yanomama took me to meet my own kind, *Nabuh,* which means foreigner, or anything that is not of their particular group or tribe. The doctors were in the area inoculating the Yanomama against Nabuh's diseases. Within a few miles of the area I was in, there were still groups of Yanomama who had not been in contact with Nabuh, and they needed to be protected from diseases brought in by outsiders. In the sixteenth century when

Nabuh first came to the Amazon rain forest, they found a thriving, social community of over five million indigenous people. But Nabuh brought disease and destruction with them in their search for gold and land. This resulted in the largest decline of an indigenous population we have ever known, leaving as few as a couple hundred thousand people scattered and isolated.

Through the two doctors I met Hoeriwe, Tuwenowa's father, a man living in two worlds. He is a respected shaman, practicing his healing arts by moving in the spirit world to rid his patients of the *Hekura* or troubling spirits that cause illness, and he also understands and works with the Nabuh's medicine, acting as a translator and assistant to the doctors. Because of Hoeriwe's understanding of my world and his own people's respect for him, I was accepted graciously into life at the shapono in Warapana, in the remote region of the Mavaca River.

After sunset at my new home, when the evening meal was completed and the youngest children were asleep, the people would gather under the open sky in the center of the shapono to dance arm in arm and to sing their heris. This joyful, playful rite celebrates life and gives thanks for life's gifts. In the deep of the night, the shaman could be heard chanting and imitating the sounds of the birds and animals living in the jungle. I did not doubt that he was in communi-cation with the flow of spirit life all around him.

Shaponos house anywhere from fifty to one hundred peo-ple, and, except for the respect offered a shaman, there is no hierarchy or political structure among the Yanomama, only family ties. To me, so many people living together in harmony in such close proximity was impressive. And although the Yanomama were first labeled as "the fierce people" by early anthropologists, they were open to me, and I felt accepted and welcome, especially by the children.

Yapapewe, a young teenager, was my first link with the children. Each morning, Yapapewe would move around the shapono singing slowly and gently to wake the extended family of about sixty people. As he circled, other young boys joined him. My first morning at the shapono, he motioned for me to follow him into the garden. All the young ones filed in behind us as we walked to the area where pineapples, papaya, sugarcane, bananas, plantains, and more are grown and harvested. I spent most of my days playing with the children while many of the women went out to fish and the men to hunt deer, armadillo, tapir, and other animals. It was the children who showed me the wonder of their jungle, brought me food, and taught me the few words of their language that I now know. My young friends were my connection with life in the rain forest—my teachers and my guardians.

Soon after I arrived, I was invited to participate in a funeral ceremony. My friends painted themselves and me with the thick red onoto seed juice mixed with ashes and stuck down feathers in our hair. We sang and danced round and round the shapono. I repeated the words of the heris as best I could, grinning at the women, who were doubled over in laughter at my pronunciation.

At dawn the next day, I was awakened by the women wailing in unison and saw the men moving together in a line waving arrows and machetes wildly as they chanted. Everyone gathered under the shapono roof, and amidst tears, the closest family of the deceased drank his ashes mixed into a soup. They believe this enables the life of their loved one to continue with them here on earth. After the drinking of the ashes, the mood softened, and people appeared at peace, feasting together on meat and fruit.

As I paddled my kayak away from the shapono, beginning the long journey back to my world, I thought about our commonly held view of the Amazon rain forest as a large green mass, critical to the stability of our global environment. Originally this area supported a thriving and healthy human community with a sustainable lifestyle. I began to see the survival of the rain forest as more a social concern than an environmental one. After all, if we in industrial nations cut down on our emissions of noxious gases, the damage to the atmosphere could be decreased just as effectively as by halting the destruction of the rain forest. How all people relate to the land and water can effect great environmental changes. And how we all relate to and respect one another is equally important. For me, the larger question of the rain forest concerns the rights we all are supposed to share: human rights. What happened to the Yanomama's rights to the land? And what happened to their rights to live as they choose in societal structures of their own making? Soon after I left, the Venezuelan government set aside a large tract of land for the Yanomama. I hope for Tuwenowa and his relatives it is enough.

— *Jan Reynolds*